STONE WALLS · GREY SKIES

BOOKS BY GEORGE TICE

Fields of Peace
Goodbye, River, Goodbye
Paterson
Seacoast Maine
George A Tice: Photographs 1953-1973
Urban Landscapes
Artie Van Blarcum
Urban Romantic
Lincoln
Hometowns

Second edition/expanded 1993
Published by the National Museum of Photography, Film & Television, Bradford, England
in association with Bradford and Ilkley Community College
(The NMPFT is part of the National Museum of Science & Industry)

Extracts from :
Antoine de Saint Exupéry : The Little Prince
JB Priestley : English Journey
reproduced with kind permission of Heinemann Ltd.

The photograph on page 81 was taken with the kind permission of the Brontë Society.

Screenplay of Wuthering Heights reproduced with kind permission of
Samuel Goldwyn Productions © All Rights Reserved

ISBN 0 948 489 14 6

STONE WALLS · GREY SKIES

A VISION OF YORKSHIRE

George A. Tice

GEORGE TICE

AFTERWORD BY JULIET R V BARKER

NATIONAL MUSEUM
PHOTOGRAPHY · FILM · TELEVISION

ALEX SMITH, SCAMMONDEN MOOR

In October of 1990, I received a Joint Fellowship from the National Museum of Photography, Film & Television and Bradford and Ilkley Community College. This involved teaching at the College, and a chance to photograph in the Yorkshire area with the resulting work to be exhibited at the Museum. The Fellowship programme was initiated in 1985 and I was to be the first American appointed.

My maternal ancestors came from the British Isles. I was named after my grandfather, George Robertson. His death certificate lists his birthplace as Aberdeen, Scotland and his occupation as basket weaver. My great grandmother, of whom I know even less, was born in Ireland. Her name was Rose Burke before she married Tom Costello. And that was the extent of my British connection.

When asked in advance of the Fellowship what kind of project I might work on, I had no preconceived idea. I consider myself to be primarily a photographer of place and my principal medium the photography book, but I had no knowledge of the North of England - what I might find there or how I would portray it. It was to be an adventure that I would respond to with a sense of mission.

The photograph on the cover of this book is a metaphor for myself, a boy cautiously crawling to the edge of the crag to peer at the valley below. I was the alien who landed on a foreign planet that my mother referred to as the 'old country'. No landscape in America that I was familiar with could I compare it to, and even the language sounded foreign.

'Old' in America meant 1940, old in England meant 1490. I had dinner near Whitby at an inn that was serving meals before Columbus set out on his voyage of discovery.

Thinking of the North of England, I think of the weather. To say it rains there isn't sufficient. To say it is cold and windy isn't strong enough. I was blown down - actually knocked off my feet - more than once. Sometimes, walking up the hill from the Museum to the nearby College flat where I resided, I've leaned forward to see if I could fall on my face but the wind kept me from doing so.

Except as a boy, and the time I served in the US Navy, I have never worn a hat. In Bradford, I bought one known as a deerstalker, the kind Sherlock Holmes wore with flaps that tie round your neck so that it cannot be blown off. It suited my idea of being British. I wore thermal underwear and many layers of clothing: shirt, pants, vest, jacket, gloves, scarf and a final layer of waterproofs, tops and bottoms. When I caught a glimpse of my reflection in a shop window I didn't recognise the bulk of my body as my own. Yet as I looked at the people about me, many were not even wearing jackets and those that were never zippered them. Young and old alike dressed that way and appeared impervious to the weather. There are only three other places where I have experienced the coldness of winter as it was there: Leningrad; the Adirondack region of New York state; and northern Maine.

That's how it was on my first visit in October through December. And on my second visit in March and April of '91, it was much the same. If asked about the rain, I'd say it rains every day - that it is always raining, or so it seems. And even if it isn't raining, that doesn't mean it won't. Should it cease momentarily, you can count on it returning. On the moors where you can see for miles, you can see it raining elsewhere. Television weathermen, when forecasting good weather, always tack on 'except in the North'. I suppose this accounts for the emerald green colour of the Dales and the roses I saw in bloom in December.

GEORGE TICE

The light changes faster there than any other place I have photographed in. Taking six frames of a subject seconds apart can produce six very different images of lighting and cloud formation. It is often dark, overcast and mostly grey. When sunshine does occur, the light is glorious and, together with the clouds, the effect can be magnificent. The sun does not arc overhead but stays closer to the horizon and even noonday light can be photographically pleasing.

It's a country of 'ramblers'. One can actually walk coast to coast via public footpaths. Private property and right of way co-exist and are compatible.

Perhaps because of the hills, I saw few bicycles, but many cars, mostly small, scaled to the narrowness of the roads and the high cost of gasoline. Crossing the streets can be treacherous. In America, one would first look left and then right before crossing. This habit must be unlearned and reversed. Once stepping into the street, it is necessary to run for safety as people drive those little cars at maximum speed and appear out of nowhere when you are half way across. They seem to drive twice as fast as prudent to get into high gear as quickly as possible. Automatic Transmissions are rare and one must become dexterous in shifting gears with the left hand. Driving on the opposite side of the road with the steering wheel on the opposite side of the car, and fear, abolished my desire to drive. Hence I did much walking and depended on others for transport.

Pubs are everywhere. The Bradford yellow pages list hundreds of them. Many are named for animals: Black Bull; Brown Cow; Red Lion; Grey Horse; White Swan. On the loneliest rural road, when you think you have reached the end of the world, there like an oasis stands a pub. Even on roads that dead end, there at the top of the hill or the bottom of a hill, is a pub. If you read one pub menu, it is unnecessary ever to read another. The half dozen meals listed are consistent with every other pub: Fish and Chips; Yorkshire Pudding; Ploughman's Lunch; Shepherd's Pie. Peas are a staple and are served at every opportunity.

There is a great shortage of ice in England. If it were possible to travel with your own supply, I'd recommend it. Many establishments have no ice and serve beverages at room temperature. I always ordered my beverages with double ice and that way I got two cubes. I think a fortune could be made there by some entrepreneur entering the ice business. At home, supermarkets sell it in plastic bags.

JB Priestley has written that there are three kinds of England: medieval, nineteenth century and modern England. Since I didn't come to England to find America, I was most attracted to nineteenth century England and the timeless landscape. Smoke stacks and church steeples are the skyscrapers of this area. Mills are ubiquitous. Many still seem to be functioning, some have been converted to uses other than the wool industry, and many are derelict.

People in Yorkshire talk of the wool trade as something that has passed. If that is so, why are there so many sheep? Could the land have supported more sheep in the industry's glory days? I was intrigued to learn that lambs are born grey and then turn white, but I still don't know why they cut their tails off. Sheep, like birds, are unusually timid and I was not able to get very close to them. Except on the Haworth Moor at Top Withins where I met a couple of meat-eating sheep who have come to depend on the sandwiches fed to them by ramblers for variety of diet.

I never saw a magpie before. What a beautiful bird, black and white with wings of blue, but so noisy. There were several nesting next to my flat and they became my alarm clock. In America, the birds start chirping at sunrise. Magpies can't wait that long and start up while it is still dark.

One of the most spectacular sights I witnessed was the starlings over City Hall - thousands of them swarming in unison, darkening the sky, blotting out the sun. They seemed so happy just being birds with nothing better to do than fly.

In Haworth churchyard, there is a rookery with many nests where I found atop a flat gravestone a dead chick that had fallen from the nest before it could fly. It caused me to consider a line from Anne Brontë's last letter to a friend after learning that she had consumption and was doomed, at twenty-nine, 'to have lived to so little purpose.' Nearby I came upon the tombstone of John Dawson Hopkins who died 'August 3rd, 1860 in the 27th year of his age'. I thought this young man must have known the Brontës. Was he a musician, or did the broken trumpet symbolise the Angel of Death sounding the last post?

Of all, or what little I have seen of England, Haworth Moor is my favourite place. Ian Colverson, of the College, introduced me to Haworth. We walked the footpaths, climbing over stone walls, past sheep, past abandoned farm buildings, to a spot where we could oversee the valley below the Brontë Falls. As he stood there, Heathcliff-like, breathing in the fresh air of the moors, happy to be away from his office, he closed his eyes momentarily and the cloud configuration merged behind him with angel wings.

After learning that Haworth was the home of the Brontës, I developed a fascination with that tragic family of geniuses. The mother, Maria, who died after giving birth to six children. The two eldest sisters, Maria and Elizabeth, who died in childhood. Charlotte, Emily and Anne, all writers of great talent. (Of the three, only Charlotte would be celebrated in her life time). Branwell, the chosen one, who could not live up to his promise. And Patrick, the father, who buried them all. If ever a story could be called tragic it is theirs.

Everything is stone. Even people are measured in stones, fourteen pounds to the stone. Stones - Stones - Stones - Stones - Stones - Stones. The cumulative effect of seeing dry stone walls everywhere you look, and realising that you have observed only a glimmer of what's out there, is overwhelming. I think of the back breaking labour in walling billions of stones up steep hills into a network of patterns over hundreds of years. There must be as many stones in Yorkshire as stars in the galaxy. If they all collapsed overnight, it would take another century to rebuild them. Rearranged, they would encircle the earth or reach the moon. They are comparable to other wonders of the world - the Pyramids of Egypt - the Great Wall of China.

In Cragg Vale, I met a dry stone waller and I stayed to watch him work. I thought there must be great satisfaction in building a dry stone wall - a thing that might endure. In Manhattan, architecture has a life expectancy of less than fifty years. He looked to be about thirty. I asked who had taught him the trade. He answered, 'No one. I taught myself.'

I watched him slowly build his wall. He hit a flat stone with a hammer and it broke into three irregular fragments. Each piece he handled, considering where it might fit. He said the process was much like a jigsaw puzzle. None was suitable for the section he worked on and so he tossed them into a pile and retrieved another that satisfied him. I pointed out that he must pick up the same pieces many times before he used them. He said that was the difference between him and a master craftsman. The master would pick up the stone once and know whether the stone fits the space.

Iselin, New Jersey
Spring, 1991

GEORGE TICE

TO HARVEY DWIGHT

Fellow photographer, collaborator, assistant, researcher, driver,
map-reader, pathfinder, pub-finder, confidant, friend. He took me
to places I had never been and only dreamed of. He brought me
closer to the elements - closer to my origins. A sprig of heather
caught between my toes and now I'm homesick. Without him
I would have been a lame duck in a sandbox.

ROAD MARKER, QUEENSBURY

CLOUDS, ARTHINGTON

On the road to Barnsley the stone walls began, settling any possible doubts. The North of England is the region of stone walls. They run from the edges of the towns to the highest and wildest places on the moors, firmly binding the landscape. You never see anybody building them or even repairing them, but there they are, unbroken and continuous from every tram terminus to the last wilderness of bog and cloud. No slope is too steep for them. No place is too remote. They will accurately define pieces of ground that do not even know a rabbit and only hear the cry of the curlews. Who built these walls, why they were ever thought worth building, these are mysteries to me. But when I see them, I know that I am home again; and no landscape looks quite right to me without them.

J B Priestley
English Journey, 1934

STONE WALLS, HAWORTH MOOR

HEBDEN BRIDGE FROM HEPTONSTALL

STREAM AND STONE WALL, CRAGG VALE

BRIMHAM ROCKS

EN ROUTE TO WYCOLLER HALL

LETTER FROM PATRICK BRONTE TO ELIZABETH GASKELL

30 July , 1855

... A circumstance now occurs to my mind which I may as well mention. When my children were very young, when, as far as I can remember, the oldest was about ten years of age and the youngest about four, thinking that they knew more than I had yet discovered, in order to make them speak with less timidity, I deemed that if they were put under a sort of cover I might gain my end; and happening to have a mask in the house, I told them all to stand and speak boldly from under the cover of the mask.

'I began with the youngest - Anne, and asked what a child like her most wanted; she answered, 'Age and experience'. I asked the next - Emily, what I had best do with her brother Branwell, who was sometimes a naughty boy; she answered, 'Reason with him, and when he won't listen to reason, whip him.' I asked Branwell what was the best way of knowing the difference between the intellects of men and women; he answered, ' By considering the difference between them as to their bodies.' I then asked Charlotte what was the best book in the world; she answered, 'The Bible'. And what was the next best; she answered, 'The Book of Nature.' I then asked the next what was the best mode of education for a woman; she answered, 'That which would make her rule her house well.' Lastly, I asked the oldest what was the best mode of spending time; she answered ' By laying it out in preparation for a happy eternity.' I may not have given precisely their words, but I have nearly done so, as they made a deep and lasting impression on my memory. The substance, however, was exactly what I have stated.

Elizabeth Gaskell
The Life of Charlotte Brontë, 1857

BUCKSTONES, SCAMMONDEN MOOR

FISHING BOATS, STAITHES

BRONTE WAY, HAWORTH MOOR

STONE WALLS, HAWORTH MOOR

WESTGATE, BRADFORD

GROCERY, HEPTONSTALL

STATUE OF QUEEN VICTORIA, BRADFORD

Not only have nearly all the big merchanting houses disappeared but a great many of the English firms too. Wool merchants, whose names seemed to us like the Bank of England, have vanished. Not one or two of them, but dozens of them. The great slump swept them away. Some of them, of course, had made fortunes before then. There were fortunes to be made in the West Riding during and just after the war. The money rolled in. I think this short period of artificial prosperity confused many people's ideas of trade. They thought, and still think, it represented some form of trading. When the slump came, many of them sat about, not bothering much and telling one another that there had been bad times before. I am no economist, but it is obvious even to me that this notion of there being a normal standard of trade is fallacious and dangerous. The situation is not merely changing temporarily all the time; it is also changing for ever. A set of conditions cannot exactly repeat themselves. The export trade of such places as Bradford was declining long before the war. We used to sell textile machinery to other countries and send out managers and mechanics with those machines. You cannot expect to teach other people to make goods and then expect them to go on still buying those goods from you.

J B Priestley
English Journey, 1934

GREENGROCER, OTLEY

STONE BARN, HAWORTH MOOR

IAN COLVERSON, HAWORTH MOOR

EN ROUTE TO WHITBY

ROOFTOPS, BRADFORD

'And what seem to you the greatest changes here?' I asked a very intelligent middle-aged woman, an old Bradford friend. She thought for a moment, then startled me by demanding, 'Where are the men?' I asked her to explain, and she continued: 'There never seem to be any men about nowadays, whatever you are doing or wherever you go. Plenty of women, but no men. It doesn't matter what it is - a dramatic society, or lectures, or at the theatre, or even a political meeting - they're all women. Where do the men go nowadays? In the old days, there used to be at least as many men interested in everything as women - it was half and half - but now it isn't. Yes, I know there was the war - but even that doesn't explain it. After all, there's another generation grown up since then. And you see the girls at everything, but not the boys and the men. What do they do with themselves? They don't go to the pubs every night, as they used to do. It's not that. It isn't even the pictures, because they're mostly women there too. Do they just sit at home and play with the wireless, or what? I tell you, it's a mystery to me, and nobody I know can explain it.'

J B Priestley
English Journey 1934

ALHAMBRA THEATRE, BRADFORD

CITY CENTRE, BRADFORD

GIBSON MILL, HARDCASTLE CRAGS

STONE WALL, HAWORTH MOOR

WHITBY ABBEY

She seated herself by me again: her countenance grew sadder and graver, and her clasped hands trembled.

'Nelly, do you never dream queer dreams?' she said, suddenly, after some minutes' reflection.

'Yes, now and then,' I answered.

'And so do I. I've dreamt in my life dreams that have stayed with me ever after, and changed my ideas; they've gone through and through me, like wine through water, and altered the colour of my mind. And this is one - I'm going to tell it - but take care not to smile at any part of it...'

'I won't hear it, I won't hear it!' I repeated, hastily.

I was superstitious about dreams then, and am still; and Catherine had an unusual gloom in her aspect, that made me dread something from which I might shape a prophecy, and foresee a fearful catastrophe. She was vexed, but she did not proceed. Apparently taking up another subject, she recommenced in a short time.

'If I were in heaven, Nelly, I should be extremely miserable.'

'Because you are not fit to go there,' I answered. ' All sinners would be miserable in heaven.'

'But it is not for that. I dreamt, once, that I was there.'

'I tell you I won't harken to your dreams, Miss Catherine! I'll go to bed,' I interrupted again.

She laughed, and held me down, for I made a motion to leave my chair.

'This is nothing,' cried she; 'I was only going to say that heaven did not seem to be my home; and I broke my heart with weeping to come back to earth; and the angels were so angry that they flung me out, into the middle of the heath on the top of Wuthering Heights, where I woke sobbing for joy.'

Emily Brontë
Wuthering Heights, 1847

GRAZING HORSE, HAWORTH MOOR

FORTUNE TELLER, WHITBY

FISHING GEAR, STAITHES

LOG OF THE 'DEMETER'

Varna to Whitby

4 August - Still fog, which the sunrise cannot pierce. I know there is sunrise because I am a sailor, why else I know not. I dared not go below, I dared not leave the helm so here all night I stayed, and in the dimness of the night I saw It - Him! God forgive me, but the mate was right to jump overboard. It is better to die like a man; to die like a sailor in blue water no man can object. But I am captain, and I must not leave my ship. But I shall baffle this fiend or monster, for I shall tie my hands to the wheel when my strength begins to fail, and along with them I shall tie that which He - It! - dare not touch; and then, come good wind or foul, I shall save my soul, and my honour as a captain. I am growing weaker, and the night is coming on. If He can look me in the face again, I may not have time to act... If we are wrecked, mayhap this bottle may be found and those who find it may understand; if not, ... well, then all men shall know that I have been true to my trust. God and the Blessed Virgin and the saints help a poor ignorant soul trying to do his duty.

Bram Stoker
Dracula, 1897

WHITBY PIER

CUTTING FROM 'THE DAILYGRAPH', 8 AUGUST

(Pasted in Mina Murray's Journal)   *Whitby*

Of course the verdict was an open one. There is no evidence to adduce; and whether or not the man himself committed the murders there is now none to say. The folk hold almost universally here that the captain is simply a hero, and he is to be given a public funeral. Already it is arranged that his body is to be taken with a train of boats up the Esk for a piece and then brought back to Tate Hill Pier and up the Abbey steps; for he is to be buried in the churchyard on the cliff. The owners of more than a hundred boats have already given in their names as wishing to follow him to the grave.

Bram Stoker
Dracula, 1897

STAIRWAY TO WHITBY ABBEY

SANDWICH SHOP, THORNTON

CLIMBERS, ILKLEY MOOR

SHOP WINDOW, HALIFAX

NORTHGATE, BRADFORD

ROOTS, BRONTE WAY, WYCOLLER

STEPS, WYCOLLER HALL

ROCKS NESTLED IN HEATHER, HAWORTH MOOR

OAK TREE, RIEVAULX ABBEY

GATE LOCK, VINCENT WHITAKER'S FARM, PONDEN MILL

VINCENT WHITAKER, PONDEN MILL

WINDBLOWN GRASS, HAWORTH MOOR

IVY BANK MILL, HAWORTH

WHITBY ABBEY AND ST. MARY'S CHURCH

CHURCH STREET, WHITBY

MINA MURRAY'S JOURNAL

Whitby

6 August - Another three days, and no news. This suspense is getting dreadful. If I only knew where to write to or where to go to, I should feel easier; but no one has heard a word of Jonathan since that last letter. I must only pray to God for patience. Lucy is more excitable than ever, but is otherwise well. Last night was very threatening, and the fishermen say that we are in for a storm. I must try to watch it and learn the weather signs. To-day is a grey day, and the sun as I write is hidden in thick clouds, high over Kettleness. Everything is grey - except the green grass, which seems like emerald amongst it; grey earthy rock; grey clouds, tinged with the sunburst at the far edge, hang over the grey sea, into which the sand-points stretch like grey fingers. The sea is tumbling in over the shallows and the sandy flats with a roar, muffled in the sea-mists drifting inland. The horizon is lost in a grey mist. All is vastness; the clouds are piled up like giant rocks, and there is a 'brool' over the sea that sounds like some presage of doom.

Bram Stoker
Dracula, 1897

COASTAL FARM, KETTLENESS

EAGLE'S CRAG, LYDGATE

ROAD FROM KETTLENESS

STAITHES HARBOUR

MERRAL'S MILL, HAWORTH

...low pressure systems conspire to change our weather back to the wet and windy type that we're all used to. That won't happen till Thursday though so its going to be a slow process, but it has started with rain down the Irish sea and in the English Channel at the moment. So I'll start today's detail in the South-East for central and southern England, East Anglia, Midlands and south east England.

It's a dull cloudy start, there is still some fog around principally in Cambridge here which will lift slowly. But it is essentially dry - some drizzle around certainly for the main rain is still in the Channel coming up from France. It will be in the southern counties fairly soon this morning, and by this evening everybody will have seen something of the rain and there will be some wet ground around. Temperatures still around the 12 to 13 mark.

Now moving into south west England, Wales, Northern Ireland, south west Scotland and the Western Isles: again a cloudy picture and there is rain in this area too - rain stretching from Cornwall, up through Wales, the Isle of Man and even into south west Scotland at the moment. And it will continue to move slowly north - the odd drop probably in Northern Ireland, nothing more than that, and south west England will also dry up during the morning with even a glimpse of sunshine there - with showers coming back later on. Temperatures around here are 12 or 13 but in the cloudier areas further north - Glasgow for example - may not exceed 11.

For the rest of Scotland and northern England it's going to be another cloudy day with little sunshine around but I think it will be essentially dry, maybe with a bit of rain on the Pennines in the morning, but it won't be till late afternoon that we really see anything really in the way of rain which will probably last into the evening and the night. But temperatures during the day are gloomy - yet again, 10 or 11. Now for a look at tonight - the showers that will be around in the south of England are likely to organize into one or two heavy ones - could be the odd bang of thunder - essentially a mild night almost everywhere. Cheerio.

JACK ROBINSON'S BAROMETER, DENHOLME GATE

LIFE BUOY, STAITHES

FROST COVERED GRAVESTONE, HAWORTH CHURCHYARD

'Good morning,' said the little prince.

'Good morning,' said the railway switchman.

'What do you do here?' the little prince asked.

'I sort out travellers, in bundles of a thousand,' said the switchman. 'I send off the trains that carry them : now to the right, now to the left.'

And a brilliantly lighted express train shook the switchman's cabin as it rushed by with a roar like thunder.

'They are in a great hurry,' said the little prince. 'What are they looking for?'

'Not even the locomotive engineer knows that,' said the switchman.

And a second brilliantly lighted express thundered by, in the opposite direction.

'Are they coming back already?' demanded the little prince.

'These are not the same ones,' said the switchman. 'It is an exchange.'

'Were they not satisfied where they were?' asked the little prince.

'No one is ever satisfied where he is,' said the switchman.

And they heard the roaring thunder of a third brilliantly lighted express.

'Are they pursuing the first travellers?' demanded the little prince.

'They are pursuing nothing at all,' said the switchman. 'They are asleep in there, or if they are not asleep they are yawning. Only the children are flattening their noses against the window panes.'

'Only the children know what they are looking for,' said the little prince.

Antoine de Saint Exupéry
The Little Prince, 1943

BARRY DAWSON AND SON, SHIBDEN VALLEY

ROOFTOPS, MARSDEN

WATERFALL, LUMB BANK

CASTLE CARR, LUDDENDEN DEAN

FOX GLOVES, LUDDENDEN DEAN

COLDEN WATERS, LUMB BANK

MORNING GLORIES, BRADFORD

LETTER FROM MRS GASKELL TO CATHERINE WINKWORTH

25 August, 1850

She is, (as she calls herself) *undeveloped*; thin and more than $^1/_2$ a head shorter than I, soft brown hair not so dark as mine; eyes (very good and expressive looking straight & open at you) of the same colour, a reddish face; large mouth & many teeth gone; altogether *plain*; the forehead square, broad and *rather* overhanging. She has a very sweet voice, rather hesitates in choosing her expressions, but when chosen they seem without an effort, *admirable* and *just* befitting the occasion. There is nothing overstrained but perfectly simple... Such a life as Miss B's I never heard of before. Lady K S described her home to me as in a village of a few grey stone houses perched up on the north side of a bleak moor - looking over sweeps of bleak moors. There is a court of turf & a stone wall, - (no flowers or shrubs will grow there) a straight walk, & you come to the parsonage door with a window on each side of it. The parsonage has never had a touch of paint, or an article of new furniture for 30 years; never since Miss B's mother died. She was a 'pretty young creature' brought from Penzance in Cornwall by the Irish Curate, who got this moorland living. Her friends disowned her at her marriage. She had 6 children as fast as could be; and what with that, & the climate, & the strange half mad husband she had chosen she died at the end of 9 years. An old woman at Burnley who nursed her at last, says she used to lie crying in bed, and saying 'Oh God my poor children - oh God my poor children!'

Elizabeth Gaskell
The Life of Charlotte Brontë, 1857

CHARLOTTE'S PARLOUR, BRONTE PARSONAGE, HAWORTH

Life in an isolated village, or a lonely country-house, presents many little occurrences which sink into the mind of childhood, there to be brooded over. No other event may have happened, or be likely to happen, for days, to push this aside, before it has assumed a vague and mysterious importance. Thus, children leading a secluded life are often thoughtful and dreamy : the impressions made upon them by the world without - the unusual sights of earth and sky - the accidental meetings with strange faces and figures - (rare occurrences in those out-of-the-way places) - are sometimes magnified by them into things so deeply significant as to be almost supernatural. This peculiarity I perceive very strongly in Charlotte's writings at this time. Indeed, under the circumstances, it is no peculiarity. It has been common to all, from the Chaldean shepherds, the 'lonely herdsman stretched on the green sward through half a summer's day' - the solitary monk - to all whose impressions from without have had time to grow and vivify in the imagination, till they have been received as actual personifications, or supernatural visions, to doubt which would be blasphemy.

Elizabeth Gaskell
The Life of Charlotte Brontë, 1857

TELEPHONE BOOTH, MIDGLEY

WUTHERING HEIGHTS

Cathy: Oh, Heathcliff, you're so handsome when you smile.

Heathcliff: Cathy, don't make fun of me.

Cathy: Don't you know you're handsome? Do you know what I've always told Ellen? That you're a prince in disguise. That your father was the Emperor of China and your mother an Indian Queen. It's true Heathcliff! You were kidnapped by wicked sailors and brought to England. But I'm glad they did it, because I've always wanted to know somebody of noble birth.

Heathcliff: All the princes I ever read about had castles.

Cathy: Of course. They captured them. You must capture one, too. There's a beautiful castle that lies waiting for your lance, Sir Prince.

Heathcliff: You mean Pennistone Crag?

Cathy: Yes.

Heathcliff: Ahh, that's just a rock.

Cathy: If you can't see that that's a castle you'll never be a prince, Heathcliff. Here... take your lance, and charge. See that Black Knight waiting at the drawbridge? Challenge him! Now charge! Charge!

Heathcliff: I challenge you to mortal combat, Black Knight!

Cathy: Oh, Heathcliff, you've killed him... you've killed him. You've killed the Black Knight.

Heathcliff: He deserved it for all his wicked deeds.

Cathy: Oh, it's a wonderful castle, Heathcliff. Let's never leave it.

Heathcliff: Never in all our lives. Let all the world confess that there is not in all the world a more beautiful damsel than the Princess Catherine of Yorkshire.

Screen Play by Charles MacArthur and Ben Hecht
Samuel Goldwyn Productions, 1939

KITE FLIERS, NIDDERDALE

VIADUCT, THORNTON

CASTLE HILL, HUDDERSFIELD

WATERFALL, HALLAS BRIDGE

FOOTPATH, HALLAS BRIDGE

ROOKERY, HAWORTH CHURCHYARD

ROOK CHICK, HAWORTH CHURCHYARD

EDITOR'S PREFACE TO THE NEW EDITION OF WUTHERING HEIGHTS

Wuthering Heights was hewn in a wild workshop, with simple tools, out of homely materials. The statuary found a granite block on a solitary moor: gazing thereon, he saw how from the crag might be elicited the head, savage, swart, sinister; a form moulded with at least one element of grandeur - power. He wrought with a rude chisel, and from no model but the vision of his meditations. With time and labour, the crag took human shape; and there it stands colossal, dark, and frowning, half statue, half rock; in the former sense, terrible and goblin-like; in the latter, almost beautiful, for its colouring is of mellow grey, and moorland moss clothes it; and heath, with its blooming bells and balmy fragrance, grows faithfully close to the giant's foot.

Charlotte Brontë, 1850

TOMBSTONE, HAWORTH CHURCHYARD

VACCARY WALLS, BRONTE WAY

RUIN, HEPTONSTALL MOOR

RAVEN STONES, WIDDOP MOOR

DAN ROBINSON, DENHOLME GATE

SHEEP, HAWORTH MOOR

HELL HOLE ROCKS, HEPTONSTALL

But there is one extraordinary thing... When I drew the muzzle for the little prince, I forgot to add the leather strap to it. He will never have been able to fasten it on his sheep. So now I keep wondering: what is happening on his planet? Perhaps the sheep has eaten the flower...

At one time I say to myself: 'Surely not! The little prince shuts his flower under her glass globe every night, and he watches over his sheep very carefully...' Then I am happy. And there is sweetness in the laughter of all the stars.

But at another time I say to myself: 'At some moment or other one is absent-minded, and that is enough! On some one evening he forgot the glass globe, or the sheep got out, without making any noise, in the night...' And then the little bells are changed to tears...

Look up at the sky. Ask yourselves: Is it yes or no? Has the sheep eaten the flower? And you will see how everything changes.

Antoine de Saint Exupéry
The Little Prince, 1943

OTLEY CHEVIN

STARLINGS OVER CITY HALL, BRADFORD

George Tice has a romantic view of Yorkshire. Not for him the dark, satanic mills or the legoland of modern industrial estates, the ungainly sprawl of townscapes. For him, it is the moorlands of the old West Riding which evoke response, and in this collection he has captured the drama of that bleak, uncompromising landscape.

It is the striking quality of each photograph which first attracts - even demands - attention: dramatic skylines thrusting against lowering skies; vertiginous hill-sides, so steep and angular that even rocks and trees seem to cling for dear life; single-tracks, carved with who-knows-what labour out of an acquisitive and hostile landscape, plunging purposefully into an unseen distance. Images such as these, their power heightened and reinforced by the severity of black and white photography, are instantly arresting and remain memorable.

Their simplicity is deceptive, however, for these images are painstakingly created by a master's hand and eye. Having attracted the eye, the photographs draw one in to observe and admire the details of composition. A dry-stone wall winding across a hillside is not simply a feature of the landscape but a sinuous extension of it, seeming to emerge from the contours of the hills. Elsewhere, a lone sheep glaring balefully into camera is apparently the subject of the study, but closer examination reveals that the shape and texture of its shaggy winter fleece is a recurring motif in the rough moorland hills beyond. These intruders have become the perfect manifestations of their environment and are scarcely distinguishable from it.

In other photographs, horizons which are otherwise empty are broken by solitary figures. A single horse grazing on a flat expanse of heath under a grey sky of banking clouds is apparently the only solid object in a scene of merging sky and land which has all the qualities of a painting by Turner.

This is in marked contrast to those photographs where the intrusion on the landscape is alien - and usually human. Where man does appear, (which is not often), he is almost invariably alone. This, George Tice seems to be telling us, is a landscape of loneliness and solitude though not of desolation. Man may stand alone in the midst of the moors but he has angel wings to support him. The timelessness of the scenery is reflected in the portraits. The photograph of the sombre urchin, armed with a handmade walking stick and accompanied by his dog, could just as easily have been taken in the nineteen thirties as the nineteen nineties. Likewise, the dour farmer in cloth cap and boots, his coat tied with string, could have been his own father, grandfather or great-grandfather. The individuals may change but the image remains the same. These are the men whose ancestors made the landscape and who today continue the struggle against nature to keep back the tide of encroaching moorland.

In Yorkshire it is rare to find a scene on which man has not left some imprint and this is reflected in George Tice's work. It is therefore surprising that where such photographs occur, they display the kind of formality which would appear man-made though it is undoubtedly natural. The magnificent waterfall at Hallas Bridge, though formed from a single river, turns into three separate falls which cascade with a complexity and symmetry of pattern reminiscent of the fountains and water-gardens of eighteenth century chateaux. The leafless branches of the rookery at Haworth Churchyard present the intricacy of a medieval cathedral window or a piece of Brussels lace. Even the rocks rearing against the skyline of Widdop Moor have a suggestion of the ruined barns and abandoned

---

JULIET R V BARKER

homesteads which litter the Yorkshire moors.

For this is the Yorkshire of the gothic novel. It is no accident that Haworth moor and Whitby feature so prominently in his collection for George Tice's photographs breathe the spirit of Emily Brontë and Bram Stoker. There are even distinct and deliberate echoes of *Wuthering Heights* in some of his compositions. The ghost of Heathcliff surely stalks the young ragamuffin playing on the rocks and the older man defying the elements on an empty moor.

The sense of confrontation which leaps out of the photographs of the countryside is not entirely absent from the urban pictures, where buildings battle for space and end up reaching for the open spaces of the sky.

Most of all, however, the urban photographs reflect a different side to George Tice - his sense of mischief. The Victorian glories of Bradford are gently mocked for their pretensions. The magnificent statue of Queen Victoria herself, presiding over a town which reached its zenith during her reign, is rendered faceless by a layer of snow as though she has drawn a veil to hide its present decline from sight. A battered stone lion, sole remnant of a prouder age, stands guard, mourning, sphinx-like, over an alien vista of modern architectural mediocrity; significantly, he has his back turned to the passing bus whose legend ironically proclaims 'on the up and up'. Even the twentieth century's grand old man of Bradford is not left unscathed: like a naughty boy, George Tice's photograph peers up the flying skirts of J B Priestley's coat.

George Tice's Yorkshire is indeed a world of grey skies and stone walls, as his title proclaims. In

JULIET R V BARKER

almost every photograph, rural or urban, moorland or seaside, the landscape is sodden with rain and the skies are clouded and storm-laden. Somehow, this seems entirely appropriate for the prevailing mood of this collection. This is a sombre, dour portrayal of a county noted for those very characteristics; it is also a celebration of the spirit and drama of a bleak, sometimes forbidding and inhospitable, countryside which nevertheless inspires passion in its admirers. In their writings, the Brontës created an evocative and lasting memorial to this landscape; in his superb collection of photographs, George Tice has done likewise.

West Yorkshire
May 1991

JULIET R.V. BARKER

Writer and broadcaster Juliet Barker was born and brought up in Yorkshire. She was educated at Bradford Girls' Grammar School and at St. Anne's College, Oxford, and from 1983 - 89 was Curator of the Brontë Parsonage Museum, Haworth. She is currently working on a major new biography of the Brontë family.

ABOUT THE AUTHOR

George Tice is acknowledged as one of America's greatest photographers of the urban landscape. Largely self-taught, his skills were noticed and nurtured by Edward Steichen, for whom he was master printer. George Tice has published eleven photographic books, and his work appears in major collections throughout the world, including the Metropolitan Museum of Art, New York; the Museum of Modern Art, New York; the Bibliothèque Nationale, Paris; and the National Museum of Photography, Film & Television, Bradford.

THE FELLOWSHIP

George Tice was the 1990/91 holder of the Joint Fellowship in Photography at the National Museum of Photography, Film & Television and Bradford and Ilkley Community College. The Fellowship is a collaborative venture between College and Museum, and exists to bring internationally renowned photographers to work and teach in the area. *Stone Walls, Grey Skies* was produced during his Fellowship year.

Edited by Penny Fell

Designed by Imelda Kay using Apple Macintosh DTP

Set in 11 on 15 point Palatino condensed 80%

Printed by Jackson Wilson on 170gms Princess Silk (acid free)

Photographic materials by Kodak (UK) Limited and Eastman Kodak

STATUE OF JB PRIESTLEY, BRADFORD